THE TALKING DAY

Michael Klein

SiblingRivalryPress

Little Rock, Arkansas
www.siblingrivalrypress.com

Sibling Rivalry Press, LLC
PO Box 27147
Little Rock, AR 72221

www.siblingrivalrypress.com
info@siblingrivalrypress.com

ISBN: 978-1-937420-27-7

Library of Congress Control Number: 2012942649

First Sibling Rivalry Press Printing, January 2013
Second Sibling Rivalry Press Printing, April 2014
Third Sibling Rivalry Press Printing, October 2014

for Eve Ensler

and in memory of Adrienne Rich

Table of Contents

THE TALKING DAY

Cartography

I'm dumb about the world. To me, it always looks haunted,
impoverished – especially in snow when it returns to black
        and white.

And sometimes I look and see nothing
but the elementary smoke rising

from a human village, over-populated,
and yet under-made. A woman from there is walking along the
        side of the road

to the next village where she can live without burning.
She's a story I make up to go with the map

Andrew shows me of a place I've never been.
Without the story, I can't make

a meaning for the flat and lettered picture of a place.
He said, he can't believe I don't just see a map

for what it is or a tree just being a tree.
And sometimes, our two spirits part exactly there.

I want to think the world moves just enough beyond
the name for what is holding it in and he wants to think it's not
        going anywhere.

He whom I made

I fell asleep in the sun and he came to me
standing on the smooth stones
in the river and asked if being human
could be made into vision: the formal
thing, not the species. Then, I fell asleep again to look for
something shining through pages of time. Some *animal*.

How to read a poem in 2013

If there's enough light
you can read anything

and don't need glasses
for the violent newsprint

or comic reliefs in bold type
running the world by accident

but mostly you don't need glasses to read the newsprint
of Bruce's new poems

in the *American Poetry Review*.
I will want to know what Bruce

has to say long after
I have listened to others who are

talking more than Bruce and what they have to say.
Bruce's poems feel as though they can't stop running because

what he remembers
and what he lives make

a double exposure and not
the usual frame around the sequence of living.

Bruce's poems face the conundrum of light behind the lines:
How do we live in the already violent world?
What do we bring to that?

They are always strong – Bruce's poems – like a man's hand
opening. Bruce's poems are: What we did to this world and what
we must do now that we've done it.

The talking day

Some lunatic with a gun killed some people at an immigration center in Binghamton, New York. Liz and her family live up there and David, her husband, teaches in the middle school which is close to all the action (the way, in any smallish town, everything is close to all the action). I called Liz to see if everyone was all right and she was in her car driving to the elementary school to pick up Lily, her young daughter she brought back from China a few years ago. Lily was fine, but Liz wanted to move her outside the question of how to make sense of the broken pieces of "someone" with a gun walking into a public space and then firing. There's something called (I learned from a news report the day of the shootings at Virginia Tech) *The Talking Day* which refers to the day immediately following the day when something wildly violent happens. No one quite grasps the reality of the situation and everyone spends that first day talking about what happened and reliving it as language – not so much to understand the violence but to make a kind of recording of it: talking about it, letting go of it, putting it down. And so I imagine it must be with Liz and Lily and David in Binghamton, New York today: letting "something" go. Liz is in her car after having just picked up Lily at school and driving back home through a town that suddenly makes no sense and she is telling the story about what happened when a young man walked into a building with a gun. And for Lily, who's had a pretty serene, un-violent United States time so far and whose endless joy has made her an adorable chatterbox, tomorrow could be her first talking day. Or if not tomorrow, some other day. We live in a talking day world.

District 9

It was a metaphor
for AIDS, for Apartheid, for the other
living on the margin – to think
they only just want to get into the place
everybody else already lives in.

There was a time,
when all revolts began,
where we lived on the margin
to state, and then to bend. To make the margin wider.

What he was reading

You are watching the wind turn pages of a book
until the weight of them stops it somewhere near the beginning.

A breath moves what the wind had in its teeth
forward to beyond the place where you left off.

You have been watching as long as
morning takes to fill in the day's picture of a man reading a book
          on a deck.

The wind won't flatter you with a future
before you finish where you are.

The wind stops on the page
you were reading before it came down to turn the rest of everything

−suspended, like a trick, as if
the book's secret isn't what you

already know, but looking down,
what you already know in the light of what you already know.

Who you loved

You want to be remembered for who you loved
and how you moved them in learning.

With each companion you marveled at the thing the partner dog
brought back.

What changed at the top of the throw to him?
What shone from the cave of his mouth?

from **When I was a twin**

Of course we knew what the other one was thinking. We were twins, weren't we? And because we were twins, how could I not know that there would be a night like this: he picks up the guy that leads to the door that leads to the stairs that leads to an unmade bed in the center of the hot night of his cold death after the stranger leaves him alone with his heart just before it jumps. How could I not know that my brother was going to be dead before I was? For every twin whose twin is dead, there must be the nagging – or is it misplaced? – grief of not being absolutely sure who to grieve, which of the two had, in fact, died? *But I was sure. Kevin was dead. I was alive. When I was a twin, Kevin was alive.*

Amazable

Who are we without wanting

anymore what we did not know?

Knowledge isn't art.

There was fire left in the paint

when Van Gogh finished the one about rain

and called it something else.

Washing the corpse

Spirit always wants the door.

After he was dead

they washed his body.

Nick and Michael and the other Michael stood in Billy's hospital room
and after whatever it was in the air stopped being there they took
the washcloth or whatever it was – something from the hospital,
something rising hot out of the silver basin – and started at his feet
and worked their way up the body that was only his body on the bed.

And Marie and Janice and Julie who had been in the room
while the spirit was directing the air had left the room so that it was
            only now
the men doing the last thing that would ever be done to Billy's body.
They were making Billy new.
They were making Billy what was over.

Ghosts

The body is everywhere.
He knew that when he let it go.

Suspend, the room said to the wire of mind as it instructed the body.
I think I see him every day: just there: at the edge of life: where it
      feels like work.

I think he comes forward through his death
anxious to mark a wall.

But I'm wrong. He wants to repeat a thing
so he can live beyond his being taken – a habit, say –

something faulty, that won't catch light.
There's Kevin, my twin brother

one day sober, trying to light a cigarette in the wind.
The body is everything.

Left to ask

I was struck today by a man and a woman in Yankee baseball clothing sitting on the shuttle train that runs from East to West on 42nd Street – the most anonymous of all train rides because we are in and out of each other's lives in one train stop. She was probably beautiful, the blond in the Yankee shirt, but tonight she had obviously been crying and her makeup was smeared and her hair was a mess from the crying but I kept thinking that maybe she had been fighting with her hair because she had to resort to beating herself up since the person she was mad at wasn't listening to her. Anyone could see he wasn't listening to her. He (her husband?) was staring off into the shuttle distance, awkwardly making eye contact with complete strangers, moving his head away from her when she wanted a simple explanation and not engaging with her on any level. And there she was – dropped from a height, it seemed, down into that garish loneliness in public that both of them may have made all the time but for this moment was a hell he had made for her to live in. All she wanted was an answer to a simple question which seemed to me when I heard it in her plaintive half-crying voice one of the hardest questions to have to ask someone who is supposed to love you: *Why won't you dance with me?* How difficult it must have been to hear a question like that and then have to give a real answer. How lonely it must be, after the ball game, to go home to a house where there is no dancing and the only question left to ask has already been asked.

My brother

What's wrong with that?
I wanted to say to him
who didn't believe the times
my brother came back inside the language
of a book or in the yellow of my living cat: Cyrus who stays
on the bed when I am leaving,
holding my brother inside because his slightest
ripple of fur would let the human out.
How can possession know how much space
it takes up in the body smaller than the one where it started
       when it was called living?

Saturn returns

Your story about your brother and his image

of God: rubber glitter of what got left when the shavings

from a pencil eraser's drawing of the sun and 10 or so

of its rays were blown away – meant he could see already

the parable of effect as I see it now after the reading

and lights for the reader: myself down here

in my fifties after a life of half remembered music listening more closely

whenever a story is this intricate, this beautiful, this fully laid down.

I wish I looked a little better, but my soul has arrived. At last.

Florida

I love how quiet and empty the streets are in Coral Gables,
which is where I am and where I have been talking to students
at the University of Miami about my writing and what I think
about queer life (marriage, bisexuality, writing objectively
about sexuality, sex and friendship). I've been to various
"phases" of Florida (which is what I think they are instead of
places because the Sun is the real place down here), and the
University of Miami campus is very beautiful because it is so
circuitous, and there is a lake and little bridges and dorms that
look like old motels and there is a swimming pool in the
middle of the campus where, in the middle of the day, people
are swimming. How strange it is to see people swimming on a
college campus – a real like-in-a-movie moment. I was hit in
every direction by how outside life is here and how cinematic.
The fact that all the architecture feels a little soulless may be
due to the presiding fact that no one spends anytime inside
except to sleep, which is still not really spending any time
inside. Inside the hotel where I am staying, there isn't nearly
as much pubescent youth as I have been seeing streaming
through campus. It's families, mostly and pre-youth
swimming in the rooftop pool, and downstairs, a woman
sitting at the grand piano in the lobby eating a sandwich. I
suppose she'd strayed in from the street. She looks like Bette
Davis in *Pocketful of Miracles*. And compared to all the vigor
of campus life, she's a reminder of the second fact of life in
Coral Gables and southern Florida in general. The sun sets.

Provincetown, 1990

We were joined that summer
in the dark
in the street of danger
and leisure against the bicycles
and the summer people – two of us loose
from that crowd back there, finding a place
in public to be alone and talking. But for me, more than
talking because I wanted you in body
and couldn't figure out how to push language through the desire
of that. I just stood still, sunburned and shuddered –
young to love, absent minded about it.
Soon, at our feet, something strange
started moving – shooting past us, very low.
Something invisible – a tube of bent air? (we couldn't have seen it)
but did see it in all its being dark and somehow see-through
that it made the street look rippled and ominous
and you said, something dark just happened, did you see it?
And of course, I did see it and in the years that have gone through
dread and anticipation lit with it, lit with summer, still see
it in different places, with different people who wouldn't
understand what force it was they were looking at – what we first saw –
that summer in the dark when it was big
and had to start through us first to get to where it was going –
        to, mercifully
be all of what it was – there, down the road a little,
where it met the world.

What I'm going to do is

I just want to follow the stranger
for awhile to see if he actually ends
up – the way the stranger you are following
must end up – in a place nobody ever sees
or ever goes to or maybe
it just isn't there at all – the place – as Rilke said
that isn't there until he's there.

At the inside pocket of the world
the stranger changes into someone
all the heaviness of following him could write: into the one
who will save us.

For he has always been the stranger.

He secretly alights!

By force.

The gifts

Everything you have is yours
except the gifts; what everybody knows; the things
the dead move around in drawers.
Those belong in the book of World All Along.

Think of it: there, on your last journey,
you let the blindfold of fear become a flag
and sailed it into the meadow of least resistance
until it got tied to the beginning.

Movie rain and movie snow

Henry James famously said that the two most beautiful words in English are summer afternoon. Let rain be next. It's been raining for two days in New York and I don't know what it is about rain in New York but it is always nostalgic. Whenever this happens I see New York through the filter of the wet weather as the place I knew in my youth. Through water I can see the buildings that are still there on 8th Street, on Lexington Avenue, in a way that I never think about when the glare of the sun points them out. Rain is the weather of memory. Rain is strange and kind. Vincent Van Gogh has a painting about rain. I'll never forget the first time I saw it at the Metropolitan Museum of Art. It's a huge painting – probably the largest canvas Van Gogh ever put paint on, and its aspect – the way Van Gogh has painted the rain – is as ethereal as it is physical. Those stabs of shortened light look as though they are trying to obscure the country as much as they are trying to bring it into focus because that's where all the motion is. Van Gogh has made a kind of still life of motion that backs up against the thing it has to absorb to be seen. But back in New York, where I live outside of Van Gogh, rain doesn't look like this. It looks, most of the time, like the rain from the last scene in *Breakfast at Tiffany's* where Audrey Hepburn is looking through a torrential episode of the stuff for the cat named Cat she just threw away.

* * * * *

It was snowing in New York – and everywhere else, apparently – but especially in New York because that's where I live and where Fifth and Madison and Lexington Avenues all run down in the same direction of snow falling on awnings and doormen and the cars and buses pulling people into jobs and schools all white morning. I love the snow because it neutralizes everything which, in this city – as generic as neutralizing may be – is welcome occasionally. I also love not being able to tell the difference between smoke and snow blowing. And there's a lot of that today. And the quiet, even in the noise. The noise of the quiet like hard thinking. Of course, I can never look or feel objective about snow after seeing *Citizen Kane* – which somewhere near the end (or is it the beginning? the whole film feels kaleidoscopic in the mind) – presents a scene in snow around the explanation for a sled named Rosebud (still vibratory in its meaning): Tyrants had childhoods.

The horse considers his music

And always, that music: at night or whatever that was rolling
over the daylashes and hitting the windows full flash with a dark mirror.

Night drops its last oat out of its last horse's mouth.

And always, this other music: in daylight when no one is close enough
to hear it because of money and the rotting earth
and the other discomforts.

Once, I heard it playing between two trees.

Everybody knows of some music sewn into life
but there is also music in the field
where I am recognized by the other horses
who come closer to the ringing ground, where the living was.

Meditation

The world writ large
is A's inner life

and sometimes mine. But mostly I run local and have
to close my eyes

to live outside of time
or feel the tugged-at thought be done

with all the entered world
or how it was before A even had an inner life coming into this
       story's life.

I don't pray. I did, but I don't now. Nothing to pray for.
No more looking for signs. One can wait forever.

But then, I'd still ask you: *Being here in broken wonder:*
is that the admonishment?

It's not our dirt

My friend at work says people look up
to see if our ancestors are close. Religion did that to the sky.
When we got to earth my friend says we needed something else
to keep us next to thinking that we sprung
from the fishes or the monkey; that we actually rose, as they say
in recovering prose, from the primordial ooze.

He says we aren't made of this planet. It's not our dirt.
Look at the pyramids (we always point to the pyramids in our
going toward the mystery) and all the other strong doses of madness
and beauty no human could have constructed but only memorialize
and canonize through time and their own brief – but for love –
time on this rented star.

I have always agreed with the voice out of the wilderness
the voice that has been looking out for us, the way that woman
in the Allan Gurganus story is *guarding the world, only*
       nobody knows.
It might as well be the alien in the kitchen
a woman in her calico, a soldier swimming in medals
threading through the pyramids: heroes
who are keeping the planet tied together.
Jesus, it has to be something like us because it isn't ...
it couldn't be ... it never was: *this* us.

A king at the door

It was 6:00 p.m. when I took the picture and I go back every
day around the same time to see if it's still there – which, of
course it is, but I mean really there – inside the frequency of
world that happens purely for the imagination: a blue
doorway with a man standing up against the door (is he
playing a horn?, waiting for his date? going over the
reservation list?) And since I took the picture and have gone
back to the picture day after day it isn't there anymore in the
actual. There are big brass doors that are closed over the
doors that are made of glass and if you didn't know where
you were you would never know the picture I took ever
existed – that there was this blue and then these shadows of
this blue beyond the big wide doors; or that a man exactly
like that stood alone in a threshold so open to the making of
meaning. I'm compulsive when it comes to images and I
don't honor their true singularity. I want to be much more –
what? – spiritual? than I am. Galen McKinley used to say,
"anything worth doing is worth over doing" and sometimes
there are days – like the first day of the blue door – when I
think anything worth seeing is worth over *seeing*. I go back
everyday to find something that isn't there because it was
there once before and had an effect on me. It took me out of
the world that never had a blue door in it. But was that
effect only a recognition of a singular beauty or was it only
important because I saw it, I put it into a photograph? Of
course, it was me, the one who took the picture of the door
with two unreadable pages of paper taped on it. And
because I could see it and know it for itself and for what it
radiated, I know there will be something else – some other
version of hidden blue; something that will catch me and

take my breath away with a glimpse into something I've never seen before. One day, summers ago, never seen before was a rectangular red and white tube that was actually a kite seemingly string-less and floating in the sky above our mystical little cottage on the beach. There's a picture of that, too: A cloud feebly knocking up against the tube, like a king at the door.

The sun in 1949

I want to start with the sun in 1949, on Fire Island, in Cherry Grove
there in the heat of desire and drinking on the dock on a speedboat,
a flag of twilight, a sandy foghorn. I want to start on the last turn

into the '50's on a ferry away from the island of industry to the island
of one sandbar and then further in to the island of night where my
mother and her mother went that summer in 1949 and drank

in the dark night of just drinking and early out to just a club
in the sand and started dancing with the same man and both dazed
in the lift away from a wood floor for awhile, both

in the same strength of searchlight stuck on him – a boy, really –
they both liked until the three of them were dancing – haunting
themselves, really – with something else and not the bodies only.

The something else got added to the waves because that was
the sound that night, the *always* sound that gets left
when the band packs up to go home – the waves and the occasional

foghorn, and some keys – keys being fumbled, keys being dropped
upon the dock. My mother and her mother were dancing
one summer night in 1949 in Fire Island and flirted twice, thrice,

four times at least but it wasn't so strict in time or could be counted
because the sex, or vapor ghost of sex threading it together made
it flirting with the same man who couldn't choose or didn't want

to choose between two women. He was a boy really who looked
at my mother and knew there was the same amount of living
in her as there was in him because they were both 17 and

there was so much more than 17 years of living inside her mother
who was 30-something and really let the booze make her dance –
sashay really – into 17 again, a spotlight away on a barroom

dance floor – and maybe it was the 17 in the 30-something year old
that this man – let's call him Joe, Joe Really – that Joe saw sex
with one eye on my mother's mother and with the other eye

on 17 years of living inside my mother who had not been given
sex at 17. My mother was waiting in the believe-it-or-not realm
of sex within a marriage. But that is my father and so far away

and here we are still stuck in 1949 – in time, really, in all the minds
present – with Joe and my mother and her mother.
And Joe allows himself now to take the two women – one woman

and one girl, really, into the site of his heart and sex and follow them
home but not all the way because he was the real 17 and would
backtrack fast the wooden plank back from the house

into the Cherry Grove where my mother – Kathryn – and my mother's
mother – Mary – lived and Joe backs off his heart but not before
he follows Kathryn and Mary into the dark shambles

of Mary's life because he cannot see where she comes from
in the arms (as it were) of vaudeville or see the film
she is in: dancing on a white piano in a sea of chorus girls

levitating on white pianos or so would rather love Kathryn
because she is 17 who won't turn into a Busby Berkeley fantasy
but will do the things that bring the family glamor down so she can

continue in life's variousnessess as Kathi who Kathryn will turn
into after Mary dies. Which is soon. But then, Kathryn did
and Mary did both love the same boy and when the boy shook

loose from the walk and the booze and the bushes that helped
make large the heated dark of confusion and passion they would
turn the night over to anger and a trip to the liquor store

and later – much later in meaning but only the next weekend –
would turn a day into the one that Mary would fly out from a
window while a psychiatrist watched across the street

from the Park Avenue apartment where her own mother lived
and flew fast to death because says Kathryn, as Kathi,
my mother, years later, it was the first argument the two

had over anything: over this boy, over this island, over this
fire which, in the talking as Kathi, my mother (years later)
was the sun in 1949 all over again.

The bed

Night for him is whatever that was in Jekyll's
beaker to bring on Hyde: alcohol, a student of the
classics will tell you.

Or was it just
all day dropping all the scenes on his heart?

There'll be intimacy,
every man says in bed.

Written in the margin of a dream

Was that sex?
Mysterious how desire leaves the body and
stands by in the years it doesn't instruct the body to draw
compassion rising like a banner from the wrecks.
There's the light of the survivors!
There! pouring out of the little radio and the other registers
        of time
onto the bed where the living was torn.

Drinking money

In 1939, when my mother was seven years old, the lyricist
Lorenz Hart gave her a photograph of himself on which he
had inscribed in midnight blue ink: *For Kathryn
Jacqueline, from Lorenz Hart, whose name will probably
be forgotten by the time she is able to read this.* Hart had
been a friend to my grandfather, a vaudevillian. My mother
kept that photograph for many years and I remember
reading it for the first time and thinking what an
extraordinary thing for someone to say to a child – as if
childhood had in it the same kind of unpredictability and
loneliness that fame did. I inherited that photograph after
my mother's death and sold it to an autograph dealer on 18th
Street in the '70's for drinking money. In the museum
of saddest things I've ever done *that* could have been the
saddest. It felt like I was making fun of beauty.

The poet

for Mary Ruefle

I'm putting your book by itself so it won't
get mixed in with the usual stuff and the other books I have
to carry around like a day laborer
who is always hungry to see something finished and only sees
the empty field with the wind thrown over it.
I've always left the game too early and can't remember now
what it was I found in a field in Bennington, Vermont
that qualified as being totally mojo enough to be used in a spell
        to make
another man love me. It didn't even work.
I was dancing then. The whole world was dancing.
Or in love with people who looked like dancers.
And you were there before your book got written.
And this idea to remain anonymous was there, too, abiding us
        with mercy.
And somebody said: *Don't get captured.*
And we looked up and said the same thing
to what we thought was the future
there, with its heartbroken electric eye, filming us from the sky.

The hoard

As if I cared enough about the things of this world and hoarded
some of the gathered and the arbitrary and took them to a place I
called the abritrarium, there was a drawer of marbles
and string and wrappers and envelopes and
toothpicks, pen knives, pens, loose change,
Tiffany blue boxes, lube, porn – all the crumbs of a
boyhood leading to when I was good, before I got lost and
claimed by the bad. This was before I acquired
      (is acquired the word?)
the fire of mind of me always standing for it.
      That was youth up in flames
in the rear view mirror of anything! poems not just read,
but lived by – seen straight through to the clearer world.
I could feel the obsession of a writer like a heat in the hand.
It doesn't happen anymore: the collection:
      the gathered or the arbitrary.
I'm the non-collector. Everything I have is already with me,
stained by me: hair and muscle and the ends
      of sentences inside an old coat,
but still the boy, I think, at silences, who smeared his own shit on
the walls and played helicopter on the edge of a Connecticut roof
until his own brother had to call and drag him off and made him
memorize it: Risk, and the "R" in risk and the "I".
It doesn't really happen anymore, and seems to me all a ruse:
      the life of the mind. What mind?
The one that's left like a shell of the one that escaped at last?
A child looks up and sneers into the thing he is holding in his hand
and shakes it up and down to make sure it has noise and lights up
and moves through his own time like no other time than this one,
like a child God in a suit of bells.
There is no past.
Nobody did anything first.
The child knows a joke he tells to the cynical sun.

There is where my sympathy comes to an abrupt end
for Bhanu Kapil

Sometimes the new dog just stands there
not looking for the toy or the small piece
of just discarded bite-sized world
and her exaggerated head is cartoonly tilted
at the lamp that is too high
even for us humans to turn on or off
and she is perfectly still in her bulldog heated heart
with the snorkeling apparatus turned off
for one startled minute – is she breathing? –
as she looks for God or some other radiant ghost we live with
and says in her own dog's
smarts: I know who I am in all of this.
My dog is a good example for me.
Everybody says that, but I really mean it.
Because I never stop long enough for exactly this tenderness
of looking because I am cruel and human and forget to take that
island in the day Jane Cooper always talked about when she
wanted me to see the moving hour through
a still life's version of it and then be moved.

Older

My knee was having a sparking feeling and I went to the doctor and found out from looking at the x-rays that my right knee has osteoarthritis. How strange it always is to see the inside of your own body, lit from behind by a light that hasn't changed through time. That couldn't be my body, I thought, looking at the simplistic black and white reverse photograph that showed how the top bone in my right knee and the bottom bone were touching each other because there's no cartilage there and how different that looked from the left knee that remains, as the nice doctor explained, perfect. Then the doctor said, listen to your body. How many times have I heard that in my life? and yet now, staring at my black and white leg, I know which part to listen to. (A lot of the other parts don't talk as loud). And it may be 20 years, but someday you will need a knee replacement, the nice doctor said. For now, it's a matter of keeping you out of pain. Then he explained the various ways I could keep out of pain and about physical therapy and about what I could and couldn't do next time at the gym. I just started with a personal trainer, too, so that was a good story to tell him at the next training session. No flying up and down the stairs, I told him. I don't have any pain – not really. Sometimes, like I said, the knee gets a sparking feeling – that twinge that never really progresses past ignition stage – but it's not really a pain, and I've had it for a few years and I'm only limping around in the morning, getting out of bed, when I feel as though everybody I've been dreaming about aren't finished telling me their stories and they're still making it hard for me to move through blessed daylight without feeling some kind of dark, some kind of pain. It's hard to stay in this body a lot of the time because it has gone through so much beauty and damage – young beauty, old damage. If only I had ... but my knee was going to fall down anyway. I feel that I've always been bearing down too hard on the right – mostly in my drunken '20's, walking horses around the barn. It's hard to look that picture of how my right leg looks from the inside knowing that it will look like this for awhile and then it will look worse. How terribly obvious injury is. It's not just the heart and mind that make us emotional creatures. It's resisting, resisting, until we absolutely have to – that staring at the bones.

Real men

The man sleeps and between his breathing
is the cat's dark version of remembered being: half-search,
half-pleasure motor assessing the flat shine fur of this life.

The man sleeps and in the hallway my dead brother
is caught in the old painting again. He hangs on the wall, happy in his chair:
social colors, Matisse-like outlines: Alexandra's version of his world

in which he's wearing sneakers painted green on the bottom and looking
at me still awake while the cat registers deeper into his purring until
he is hunting with his mind and the man begins the see-saw breath

of joy and danger – day and night – he loves me not – asleep. We had a
fight I think but the fights stack up like white plates in the dark cabinet and
all look alike by now. And sound alike too, as if he's going back for the

language he wanted to chide his earlier lover for that strange showcase
of being in a relationship: long table fully set in a dining room: elegant
but for no one and when every other room in the house was a mess.

And the man remembers and will say it to me rearranged as now for the
fight in this relationship that I live a disordered life. And it is disordered
and I'm older than most of the people I love and every pain is finite

and has a chair and sometimes I sit in one of living's chairs to look down at
what happened to me one night from the '70's: tossed out of a bar
for no reason: waking up in the bloodied fun house mouth of a doorway:

both eyes shattered with dawn but happy that I could still move barely
into 9th Avenue's light. We both go back to varying scenes from two lives
of single inventions into this night of life that invented a stately chase

and let us be in this city with this cat and these paintings barely still
depicting worlds in a hallway. I can never get to sleep like this: the past
caught up to darkness vibratory; silence next to that when the man stops

counting and the cat rustles like a nightly hero in a running dream.
They're done. I have to finish the fight in my head, by myself. And look
at the man once more to make sure it is him. And enter the night unarmed.

Love poem for the one I later found sleeping

I'm moving away from one story of
who I am and into a night
from the 70's rain coming down
like weeping again over mostly
weeping Hell's Kitchen in a resin
glowing so late it's early and no one
is left in the world if this were a movie.

I should have told him Yeats and his *do not love too long*
and should have kissed him then.
I should have kissed Gordon
who would not have given me his heart
and so, too, would not tell his soul.

Caleb

Caleb had to be put down today because he got diabetes and
we couldn't get his sugar down and he was pissing all over
our apartment and we went in and out of dealing with it as
best as we could and then not dealing with it because our
lives were getting overturned and Andrew was dealing with
it more than anybody was dealing with it because he was
home with it because he's not working now and that cloud of
not working and the cloud of Caleb changing day by day
hour by hour made us call the vet and she supported the
decision of letting Caleb go out of this world and then he did
go out with her support so quietly with his paws wrapped in
his Caleb way around Andrew's arm and left us and left
Andrew in the first minute of a different world with an
empty carrier to take home. I said to Andrew hours later it
may have been better just to take him over the vet in his wild
nature not in the carrier because as Andrew's friend Greg
pointed out he would have to take the empty carrier home.
And he did. He carried the carrier which was lighter now all
the way home. And Cyrus was there – Caleb's brother who
until now has been with Caleb every minute of every year
that added up to eight years and now is alone and when we
aren't there he will be in the alone of the alone – the alone
that is the same as where people are when they are alone:
nothing in the way to see the open Caleb-less road. I wonder
what Cyrus will find in the world without his brother? And if
he will bring it back to us. Please bring it back to us Cyrus
whatever it is.

Politics

They want me to talk. My voice
is back and they want me to tell them
how it really happened. In my voice, apparently,
what really happened sounds different
once it is heard, unpacked from its box of voices.
My voice makes anything I say sound like something
I just found out. And probably,
hazardly, maybe, and troubling, of all the voices in this unnerving
world, they want me to use mine, the man and the woman who
are telling me all this with their heads in the open window
this voice, the one that is awake now and living outside of its box
tell them certainly how it is, and who the people are,
and how it really happened,
and what they're going to have to do now,
now that they've heard my voice saying
what it can never say even when it is talking.

The same dream

Every night for months I've had a variation of the same dream.
I'm in a school. I'm the teacher.

The dream world comes and sits in a room.
We are speaking in a language that no one has heard before
but which everybody understands.
Welcome dream world.

There is a moment of a high wind blowing
and a moment of sunlight brightening more of the branches and
making the scene hard to see.
Inside the fold of sun and wind there are more women than there
        are men.
Then, there is an animal – usually a four-legged animal.
At some point in the dream somebody always comes back to life.
At some point in the dream somebody doesn't come into the room.

City, city

When the dog looks at her human who is in his downward
          dog position
I wonder if this will be the day I find out
what that clicking thing in my body is – knocking on a variety
          of places
doing something important in my throat, turning my knee
to the left, keeping me maybe, from the rest of my
          body's offering.
I'm a bad student of living. Cynical.
I don't know where the yoga goes
I've been waiting too long for peace
at the dark theatres of afternoons with movies or the books that
are being written now in which a stranger comes into view and
invariably settles on a city because a city
itself is a fuse life pushes into a box on the world.

The radiant

To go to the Russian baths on a whim –
which is what Matthew and Shane and I just did –
is sort of like getting on the Staten Island Ferry on a whim –
which is what Nina and I once did in my first body's world of
girlfriends and high school voice classes: the terrifying *Carmina
Burana* and then Shubert's haunted song cycle *Winterreise*
and its songs for the haunted postman, the haunted raven.
How did I ever survive my own singing? and still sing –
or did we walk? – the unknown Staten Island until
it came up short at the burned out house where some clothes
got left and where as a kind of praise to SURVIVE
we took ours off and put on some others that the fire didn't want.
Then we got back on the ferry which in my mind
charged ahead in the story and took 30 years to get to this night's
whim which is the opposite of Staten Island, the opposite of Nina, is
radiant heat or icy water or propelled mint air rolling in steam along
          some classic tiles.

*My mind broke into a hundred images for pleasure until
my body: cave around a stove – was actually there.*

And there again: in the past again but forward, where the poem
          just started –
this time a fallen night's flash in the eye of a sequined hem: I'm next
in line for sex in the 70's: TONIGHT at the Club Baths:
          drunk probably,
noticeably probably, down to my last admission money loving on
          some weekend
Texan who thinks New York has always been Warhol's city,
Warhol's war cry. OPEN CITY: I tell him. I tell him: wear my body.
I am in the world as object and tonight I meet my body again in the
second world of my body: utilitarian and nobody else's.
I am remembering my body in time.
It has so many movies in it, so many last scenes.

My body has people leaving a theater in it.
My body is of the tribe: not queer, not current, not desirous
        of anything
except – is this relief? – what comes on by degrees.
I am trying what's left of my health in a certain temperature.
        And trying it again
in another room. Lady Lazarus's heart comes to me suddenly:
        it really goes.
And then, just as suddenly something I would
never say: *I am Radiant. I am in radiant's hand.*

The track

i

There's a sacred place on the FDR Drive
where a car can be the eye inside the East
River and the future of traffic and water
is the way upper left of what if this was a painting and I was
        alive in it.

But instead of mortal cars into the sky, I am thinking
of the racehorse and what seeing means in his life
and if this were his race he would know that desire holds
        more than time which is why
someone in the human class is always on a kind of rail to
        watch him.

ii

Things I didn't do when I lived on the racetrack:

read books
look at stars
call somebody
see a movie
see a play
get in a car
look at stars
call somebody
write a letter
walk into a store
eat vegetables
eat fruit
use a pen
look at stars

call somebody

Things you didn't do:

look for me

iii

the prophecy: you'll remember a trip south;
the woman you went to live with for awhile;
the woman you told cancer
when you didn't have cancer. On the racetrack you said
you were dying of the current dying
because you didn't know how else it could be understood:
        what nobody
can say: *I am living of something.*

The train prayer

I am almost completely happy
beyond the future beyond the future beyond the future
We drag history around like the wild west show.
Or the animal loved once and then shunned,
wanting nothing but the still waters
of shall we gather at the river, the beautiful, beautiful river.

The hand

My right hand for a long time has felt as if it is trying to wake up
from a dream: numb and then suddenly startled awake
like being pushed against a dressing room door's star.
It's gone by midday and later, I always have to remember what it was.

I type the poem or the email. I'm in the future. I move the hand again.
The hand is in revolt against whatever it almost told me when it was
trying to wake up. I don't know anything. I am a child who makes
things with his hands. I don't know what else my hands are for.

What it was like to have written

Then, he asked me if the I in the poem is always me and if
poetry is how the I is not necessarily the real I. And I told him
the I is always the I in my poems unless of course
I am using an I I want back that isn't for anybody. The other I.
The I that doesn't know from poems.
Then I said, but that doesn't necessarily go for the He.
The He isn't always you I said to him after I showed him the poem
I wrote with the He in it and some other examples of He things.

What happened

Direct sunlight.
Shadow of him, next to shadow of a dog.
The rest of light waits somewhere he's been to
And never thought he'd have.
Here in beyond – a little – the middle of his life.
The ocean, a success behind that.
He knows what happened.
He asked for love.
That was his first mistake.

Image results for the sky

Last night's dream opened with me and Andrew lying in an inflatable boat on some body of water somewhere in summer. A plane was slowly falling out of the sky and heading right towards us. I remember thinking in the dream (when thinking feels like you're pulling on the length of a telescope) that I'd seen this before: a plane falling, floating almost, towards these two men in this boat. Then it stopped and Andrew instinctively knew nothing was going to happen to us. Later that same day or year of the dream, I am in a house with a lot of people hanging around – all age groups; a house with a porch in the country and the air is very still. It's night and a young man is reading me a poem he wrote and asks me what I think of it and I secretly hate it but of course I don't tell him that. I tell him it feels like the beginning of a poem. I tell him there's no ghost poem and that every poem has a ghost poem – which upon waking, is an idea I don't know whether is true or not. I'm reading a book by Charles Baxter about subtext and the ghost idea, I'm sure, came out of that book. Suddenly, in the night of the dream, the sky starts this incredible light show – kaleidoscopic, slightly frightening – all about reminding the town enthralled below that the sky is a screen for the world without a projector. It tells us what it wants to tell us. Then, someone else reads a poem again, which is a better poem than the first poem.

* * * * *

We're at the beach. Everybody is at the beach. It's summer, in the first turn. And Jean is there and me and Andrew and

a slew of beautiful boys – beautiful the way they were at the
beginning of liberation when all the queers looked like
hippies. And there's a car (there's always a car) and the guy
I'm with (there's always a guy), is driving it the other way –
actually sitting the other way – looking at where we were
instead of where we're going. Miraculously, we get there –
the part of the dream that feels goal oriented. But I don't
know what we're there for exactly, unless it's for sex which,
in a lot of dreams – my dreams anyway – it is. There's a
carnival on the dream beach. In the rooms that border the
beach women are painting floors and making flags and
nobody (suddenly in the middle of the dream) is there that I
know and my cell phone (which the dream has decided to
make an old sneaker) splits in half and I'm thinking that
Andrew will do everything he can to find me or at least take
me somewhere where I can get another phone. But where
we are, where I am in my dream, makes it very clear that
even though there are houses and the natural world at the
intersection of so many people talking and being in so much
summer there is nothing like money or goods. There is as
there always has been what we have made and what we
brought with us. There is only what we can carry. I'm doing
a reading that night and so is Jean but in different places
and I don't know how to reach her or Andrew or the vague
choir of boys swimming in my mind or why I even need to
reach the vague choir (except for another fix of beauty). And
I'm suddenly thinking mundanely (the way a schedule feels
mundane and sharp in a dream), who will I have dinner
with? And so I just start walking, broken sneaker in hand,
down a street of trees, trees, the first trees all day, their first
appearance in the dream. And I see a woman dressed up for
a performance of some kind because she is carrying a
trumpet in a leather case and is dressed in that way

musicians who play classical music get dressed – between inspired and formal, black usually with sneakers – and I say, *I know you* and she says, *I know you* and then she says, Lisa Epstein, Music and Art and I say, that's right, and then I say, Michael Klein. And I wake up to Saturday's unexpected sunlight into Andrew into the world I always leave to go dream walking and I tell him about my dream and how sad I was that I couldn't find him at one point that I didn't know where he was. And Andrew looked at me in this life with his eyes closed and said *I was there* – and then with that Grapes of Wrath sort of intention – *I was there behind the tree.* Andrew said *I will always be there, behind the tree, looking out for you.*

Acknowledgments

Some of these poems and prose poems, at times in different form, appeared as follows:

Fence: "Image results for the Sky," "Drinking money"

Assaracus: "Washing the corpse," "Amazable," "Ghosts," "District 9," "How to read a poem in 2013," "The bed," "The same dream," "Politics"

Tin House: "Real men"

Ploughshares: "Cartography"

Post Road: "Provincetown, 1990," "What I'm going to do is"

The Awl: "What he was reading"

Lumina: "The hoard," "Saturn returns," "The radiant," "The poet"

Court Green: "What happened," "There is where my sympathy comes to an abrupt end"

BLOOM: "The sun in 1949," "The talking day"

"Caleb," "The talking day," "Movie rain and movie snow," "Left to ask," "Older" first appeared in *States of Independence*, winner of the inaugural *BLOOM* chapbook contest for non-fiction (judged by Rigoberto Gonzalez)

About the Poet

Michael Klein's previous collections of poetry include *then, we were still living* (GenPop Books, 2010), a Lambda Literary Finalist, and *1990* (Provincetown Press), which tied with James Schuyler's *Collected Poems* to win the award in 1993. Additional work includes *The End of Being Known* (University of Wisconsin Press, 2003) and *Track Conditions* (Persea, 1997). Recent work appears in *Tin House*, *Ploughshares*, and the *Ocean State Review*.

About the Press

Founded in 2010, Sibling Rivalry Press is an independent publishing house based in Little Rock, Arkansas. Our mission is to publish work that disturbs and enraptures.

CPSIA information can be obtained
at www.ICGtesting.com
Printed in the USA
FFHW020342061119
55931849-61800FF